068959

All-American Fighting Forces

WASPs

JULIA GARSTECKI

WORLD BOOK

This World Book edition of *WASPs*
is published by agreement between
Black Rabbit Books and World Book, Inc.
© 2017 Black Rabbit Books,
2140 Howard Dr. West,
North Mankato, MN 56003 U.S.A.
World Book, Inc.,
180 North LaSalle St., Suite 900,
Chicago, IL 60601 U.S.A.

Design and Production by Michael Sellner
Photo Research by Rhonda Milbrett

Library of Congress Control Number: 2015954921

HC ISBN: 978-0-7166-9658-2   PB ISBN: 978-0-7166-9659-9

Printed in the United States at CG Book Printers,
North Mankato, Minnesota, 56003. PO #1794 4/16

Contents

CHAPTER 1

Fly Girls

Deanie Parrish pushed her B-26 **bomber** faster. A **gunner** in a B-24 trailed her. He sprayed her plane with bullets. Two bullets hit their mark. Parrish had to land.

Parrish flew like she was in battle. But she was really training. She was helping another American pilot practice.

Being a WASP

Parrish was one of the Women Airforce Service Pilots (WASPs). She helped male pilots train for war. Being a WASP was dangerous. WASPs flew broken planes in for **repair**. Male pilots practiced by shooting at them. And they flew when many people thought women shouldn't fly.

WORLD WAR II PLANES

U.S. pilots flew more than 70 different aircraft during World War II. WASPs flew them all.

B-29 Superfortress
Top Speed: 358 miles
(576 km) per hour

A-20G Havoc
Top Speed: 317 miles
(510 km) per hour

Wing Span:
141 feet, 3 inches (43 m)

Wing Span: 61 feet, 4 inches (18.7 m)

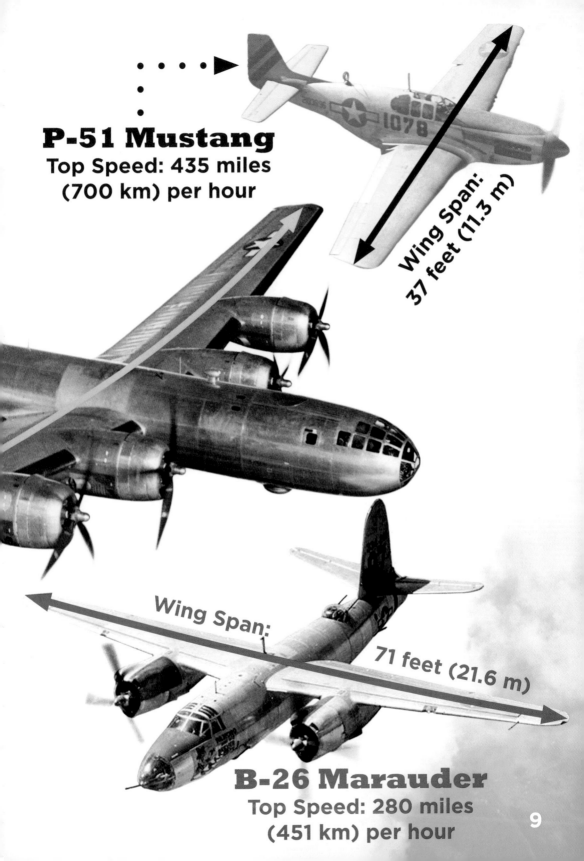

P-51 Mustang
Top Speed: 435 miles
(700 km) per hour

Wing Span:
37 feet (11.3 m)

Wing Span:
71 feet (21.6 m)

B-26 Marauder
Top Speed: 280 miles
(451 km) per hour

CHAPTER 2

Joining the

The United States entered World War II in 1941. Female pilots wanted to join the Army Air Force. But they were not allowed. Officers didn't think women could be military pilots.

Some female pilots flew to Great Britain. They joined a British women's pilot group.

Letting Women In

By 1942, the United States needed more pilots in battle. The Army Air Force finally agreed to let women in. But women could only help male pilots. They could not fly in battles.

Women in World War II

more than 1,000 WASPs

more than 10,000 Coast Guard Women's Reserves

14,000 Navy Nurse Corps

23,000 Marine Corps
Women's Reserve

more than 150,000
Women's Army Corps

about
358,100
total

60,000
Army Nurse Corps

100,000
Navy's Women Accepted for
Voluntary Emergency Service

WASPs Training in WWII

women applied
were accepted
earned their wings

0

Training

Many women wanted to join the pilot program. Only a few were chosen. To be picked, the women had to be pilots already.

In training, they learned about weather and map reading. Then they learned to fly every kind of military plane.

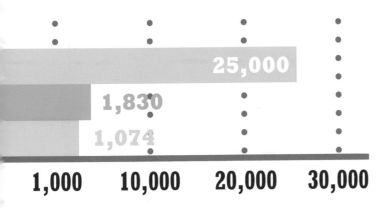

25,000

1,830

1,074

1,000   10,000   20,000   30,000

CHAPTER 3

Doing

WASPs flew many **missions**. They picked up new planes from factories. Then they flew them to male pilots for use in battle. They also flew broken planes in for repair. It was dangerous flying broken planes.

Brave
Pilots

Helping Train

WASPs also helped train soldiers for war. They sprayed **tear gas** on ground soldiers. The soldiers practiced putting on their gas masks.

WASPs also pulled targets for shooting practice. Men on the ground shot live bullets at the WASPs' planes.

Flying the Big Planes

Some male pilots felt a few planes were not safe. For example, the B-29 was a large plane. Some men felt it was too heavy. WASPs flew B-29s without problems.

WASPs
BY THE NUMBERS

1,102
TOTAL WASPs

12,650
AIRCRAFT DELIVERED

38 WASPs DIED WHILE FLYING

120 NUMBER OF U.S. AIR BASES VISITED

17 MONTHS THE PROGRAM LASTED

60,000,000 MILES (96,560,640 km) FLOWN

CHAPTER 4

Ending the Program

By 1944, the military didn't need as many pilots for battles. Male pilots began coming home. They took back their old jobs.

The WASPs had excellent flight records. But they were still sent home.

Women Pilots
in the Military

WASP
program
1,102
pilots

2015
678
pilots

Leading the Way

The WASPs proved women could fly as well as men. But the military still wouldn't let them fly. Today, women can fly in the military. The WASPs are remembered for leading the way.

DECEMBER 1941

The United States enters World War II.

MARCH 1942

Women go to Great Britain to fly missions.

1940   1941   1942

SEPTEMBER 1942

U.S. military allows female pilots to join.

AUGUST 1943

Two groups of female pilots join together. They become the WASPs.

DECEMBER 1944

WASP program ends.

1943

1944

1945

JUNE 1944

Congress refuses to keep WASP program.

SEPTEMBER 1945

World War II ends.

GLOSSARY

bomber (BOM-uhr)—an aircraft made to carry and drop bombs

Great Britain (GRAYT BRIT-uhn)—an island west of Europe that includes the countries of England, Scotland, and Wales

gunner (GU-nur)—a soldier who operates a large gun

mission (MISH-uhn)—a job assigned to a soldier

repair (ree-PAYR)—to fix something that's broken

tear gas (TEER GAS)—a gas that makes a person's eyes fill with tears; it's often used to break up large groups of people.

BOOKS

Adams, Simon. *World War II.* Eyewitness Books. New York: DK Publishing, 2014.

Lukesh, Jean A. *Sky Rider: The Story of Evelyn Sharp, World War II WASP.* Grand Island, NE: Field Mouse Productions, 2011.

Thompson, Ben. *Guts & Glory: World War II.* Guts and Glory. Boston: Little, Brown, and Company, 2016.

WEBSITES

Female WWII Pilots: The Original Fly Girls
www.npr.org/2010/03/09/123773525/female-wwii-pilots-the-original-fly-girls

National WASP World War II Museum
waspmuseum.org

Women Airforce Service Pilots (WASP)
www.thestoryoftexas.com/discover/campfire-stories/wasp

INDEX